Jenni Wakes Up!
Stephen Bradley Archer

ISBN 979-8-89569-125-0

I dedicate this enlightenment to
all of those who have been a light
in my journey

Shannon - my true Light

Dee - for opening the Door

Patti - for mentoring my Path

Jamie - providing Inspiration
and Truth

Jenni .... it's time!
Jenni it's time to wake up!
Jen-n-n-ni!

Chapter One – Jenni Wakes Up

Just like every other morning nothing seemed special about this morning. It was October which is Jenni's favorite month. Leaves on the trees always were their most beautiful this time of year, especially the large maple tree right outside Jenni's bedroom window. Jenni always liked wearing her favorite colorful sweaters in the fall.

On sunny mornings the sunlight always came in through her bedroom window. The beams of golden light shining through her window creating rainbow reflections. The rainbows of light moved throughout her bedroom as the rays of light gleamed through the crystals that she had hanging from her window sill that her Grandma had given her.

"Ohhhh - Boy!" Jenni said with a big waking yawn while trying to remember a night of wonderful dreams. Lying still with her eyes closed, Jenni tried to remember her dreams the best she could. Thinking back to her last night's dreams, she remembered that she and her little brother Bobby were playing in the park with Grandma Patti and with their new puppy. Jenni thought how much fun she and her Grandma would have together. But now their puppy wasn't a puppy anymore like in her dream, but now was a full-grown smelly dog.

Thinking of her dream, Jenni smiled and let out a little laugh as she jumped out of bed to get ready for school. She could smell the delicious aroma of the breakfast her Mom was preparing downstairs.

Being in such a rush she almost forgot to brush her teeth but remembered at the last second how Grandma always talked about how important it was to brush those "pearly whites." Jenni missed her Grandma terribly ever since she passed away last year, but always felt that Grandma Patti was still around and close by in some way. Jenni and Grandma Patti had a very special relationship. They were very close and spent a lot of time together. Everyone would tell Jenni that she looked just like Grandma Patti when she was a little girl. They liked the same foods, liked to wear the same colors of clothes, and had the same beautiful smile that brightened up the room.

They were like the best of friends and always together.

She could hear her Mom call up the stairs from the kitchen, "Jenni, get your brother and come down for breakfast or you'll be late for school!"

Running past Bobby's room Jenni knocked on his door, "Bobby come on, we are going to be late!" Jenni called out. Jenni could hear Bobby playing and talking to his imaginary friend Stephanie again through the crack in the door. "Come on Bobby, tell Stephanie you'll play later when you get home from school."

As a daily game she jumped down the stairs, trying to jump past as many steps as she could to see if she could make it down without ever touching the one step. To Jenni, jumping the stairs reminded her of sometimes in her dreams where she could fly above the trees of her neighborhood and visit far off places and have adventures.

She loved those dreams. Jenni never teased Bobby when he played with his imaginary friend. Jenni remembered she too once had an imaginary friend when she was little. But she was a big girl now and big girls don't have imaginary friends, at least that is what her big brother Kevin would tell her.

Jenni could smell the smell of her favorite breakfast food drifting down the hallway as she made her way to the kitchen. Pancakes! Something that Jenni was always capable of doing was recognizing certain smells that would remind her of special moments, especially those smells surrounding Thanksgiving and Christmas.

Mom and Grandma always seemed to be baking special treats for the family during those special times. Those wonderful smells and moments made Jenni's family time during the holidays very special. Even when it was summer, there were times she would believe that she could smell pumpkin pie or Christmas cookies somewhere in the house.

"Pancakes!" Jenni shouted, "my favorite!"

Sitting down at the breakfast table, she began to gobble up her pancakes, drink her milk and think about nothing else but how wonderful the pancakes were.

Bobby had finally made it down the stairs by then and right before he sat down, Jenni moved Bobby's glass of milk to the center of the table. She didn't know why she moved the glass, something inside her told her in an instant, "You better move Bobby's glass!" It wasn't an out loud voice that everyone could hear, but a little voice inside her head and feeling from inside her stomach letting her know to move the glass.

"Geezzz! Bobby be more careful, if I didn't move your glass you would have spilled it all over the table and floor." said Jenni.

Chapter Two – Off to School

 "Off to school now you two, you don't want to be late!", Jenni's mom said as she gatheredup their school bags, "And wear a warm coat, it's supposed to be cold today." Jenni slipped on her coat and wool hat from the hallway closet. Opening the front door Jenni and Bobby were off, down the front porch and headed to school with the rest of the neighborhood children that were making their way down the sidewalk.

 Jenni's school was not that far away from her house. The school was just a couple of blocks away. Jenni always liked walking to school with her friends where they could talk about things they did after school and wonder what their teacher had planned for them to do during the week. There was one main street that everyone had to cross that was a very busy street on the way to school. There was a crosswalk light at the corner, but sometimes the cars would race through the crosswalk trying to beat the traffic light. Jenni came to the crossing and waited for the "walk" light to turn on. When the walk light came on and it was okay to cross, she still looked both ways before crossing.

 "WAIT!" a little voice inside her said. Jenni also had that funny feeling again that something was about to happen. As everyone was about to cross, Jenni called out for everyone to wait. Just then a car, that was in a real hurry, raced through the red light and through the crosswalk. "Wow Jenni how did you know? We never saw that car coming even after looking both ways." Jenni's best friend Dee said. "I don't know Dee, something made me think that everyone had to wait." Jenni said.

The rest of the school day was normal,
and nothing really happened until...

"Pop Quiz!" Jenni's teacher Mrs. Jamie called out to the class. Mrs. Jamie handed out the quiz to all the children. It was a math quiz.

"Ugggh!" Jenni said softly with a low groan.

Math was not her best subject, and she always had trouble doing math. Jenni placed her elbows on the desk with her fingers in her hair staring down at the quiz thinking that she would never be able to get these problems right.

As Jenni stared at the paper thinking it was going to be impossible, she remembered something that her Grandma Patti would always tell her to do when she was having trouble finding answers to any problem that she was having. When you are having trouble finding an answer, put your hands in your lap, close your eyes and take three long breaths. The answer will come to you. Placing her pencil down on the desk, Jenni placed her hands in her lap, closed her eyes and took three long breaths. She took another long breath in through her nose and held it in for a bit and then let it out through her mouth.

After doing this simple task, she imagined that she already knew the answers to the quiz and that she simply had to write the answers down. After sitting still for a couple more minutes, Jenni opened her eyes and was fully relaxed and ready to start the quiz. As Jenni went through the questions on the quiz, the answers seemed to pop out of nowhere and she was able to answer every problem without any doubt that she got them right. Jenni finished the quiz and placed it on the teacher's desk as the school bell rang sounding the end of the school day

Jenni met Bobby outside on the school playground, and they walked home paying special attention to that busy crosswalk.

When they got home Jenni and Bobbie did their after-school chores. It always felt good to help their mom around the house. They helped clean, pick up things, rake some leaves in the backyard, and helped doing the dishes after dinner. After dinner Jenni and her family would play games, read or just sit and talk about what happened during the day at school. That was of course if they didn't have homework, that always came first.

Jenni loved the family time they spent together and sometimes it seemed like she could smell those warm cookies that Grandma used to bake when everyone was together laughing and having fun in the house.

It was getting close to bedtime, so Jenni got ready for bed. Jenni's mom came into Jenni's bedroom as she always did at bedtime. Jenni loved to be tucked in. "Now have sweet dreams and try to remember your dreams and tell me all about them in the morning at breakfast," Jenni's mom said as she leaned over kissing her on the forehead.

Jenni rolled over as she looked at the moonlight shining through the window. The beams of moonlight shining through the crystals in the window made it seem as though there were stars shimmering all around her bedroom.

Jenni closed her eyes and fell fast asleep from a wonderful day

Chapter Three – Awakening

As Jenni drifted off to sleep, she suddenly has the sensation of standing at the edge of a beautiful forest meadow. In her dream she could see a flowery meadow with a small clear winding stream.

Jenni listened to the sound of the water traveling along the riverbed rocks. She watched the floating leaves drift by that had fallen from the trees that surrounded the mountain meadow as she stood by the edge of forest's tree line. Jenni thought to herself that it seemed that somehow, she had been to this place before. There was a loving sense of belonging and comfort. The last thing she remembered was getting ready for bed and then suddenly in a moment she is standing at the water's edge by the meadow. An overwhelming feeling of joy and warmth filled her heart.

" Jenni," she heard someone call her name softly". Jenni, I am so glad you are here," the familiar voice said once more. Jenni turned slowly to the direction of the voice."Grandma!" Jenni whispered to herself. "How can you be here and how did you find me? Where are we?".

     "You are at your dream journey's starting place. This is the place in your dreams that you come to start your night's dream journeys. It is also the place that you can come to anytime just by closing your eyes, settling yourself and concentrating on your breathing and listening to your heartbeat. Also, by taking time to focus on your heartbeat and to your Higher Self," Grandma Patti explained.

     "What is my Higher Self mean Grandma?" Jenni asked.

     Jenni's Grandma went to explain that a person's Higher Self is your full Soul Spirit. While you are living as a human and experiencing things in your current human body, known as Jenni, it is but a small part of your full Higher Self's Soul Spirit. Imaging your full Higher Self's Soul Spirit is like a rainbow sun that contains all the colors that you can imagine, and it also contains those colors that you can't imagine. Now out of all of those millions and millions of colors, let's imagine one color, say a light pink. Now there may be many shades of light pink, but let's just pick one shade of a beautiful light shade of pink. This light shade of pink that you have imagined is now you. A light that is shining down on the earth as you are living your life as a little girl named Jenni. Even though you are living down on the earth as this beautiful light shade of pink named Jenni, you are always connected to your full rainbow circle of light of every color.

     This is how you are always connected to your full Higher Self's Soul Rainbow Spirit.

To connect to your Higher Self anytime, just imaging traveling up the light pink beam of light back up to your Higher Self's rainbow circle of every color.

"Jenni, there is something that I am going to tell you that is very important and once you understand what I am about to tell you everything will become clear. I have so many other exciting things that I can't wait to tell you as well." said Grandma Patti.

Jenni squinted her eyes, stuck out her neck forward, turned her head sideways just a bit and opened her ears as wide as she could to listen very carefully to what was to come next.

"Jenni, everything you can see, hear, touch, smell, and feel is alive and made of energy. Everything in the whole Universe is made of some sort of energy and everything is connected to everything. You have the power to take in energy from things around you to help you feel better and happy.

Do you ever wonder why when you are at the park playing barefooted in the grass among the trees and people that you feel happy, loved, and full of life? This is because you are connecting to all the energy of the things around and you are receiving the love and light energy from everything around you.

It is also important that you share your own loving light energy back to the plants, animals, and people around you to increase their loving energy as well. This sharing only increases to the whole positive loving light energy of the planet and universe for all to share."

"Ohhhh, but why do I feel sad or afraid sometimes?" Jenni asked.

That's a very good question Jenni," Grandma Patti replied.

"Sometimes there are negative feelings, bad things that happen, or even people that when we are around them that do not make us feel very happy or positive. There are people that like to take the positive energy from you and not give anything back in return. Let's imagine that your heart is a box and the box is just so big that you can only fit so much into it. The trick is for you to fill your heart box with only positive loving light energy and not place any negative or bad things into your heart box.

This doesn't mean not to remember those things that make you feel sad or unsafe. This means not to let those negative feelings or bad dark energies in to fill your heart box. The best thing you can do to turn bad negative dark energy back into positive loving energy is to send those feelings, things, or people positive loving energy."

"There is an old Hawaiian expression that you can use to send out positive loving energy and forgiveness, and that is by saying - Ho'ohponopono! (Ho-oh-po-no-po-no)

Expressing this loving energy thought to those negative dark energies is explained in the following translation – 'I'm sorry, please forgive me, thank you, and I love you.'

Using this simple expression of sending loving light energy out to the world and universe will fill your heart box with pure positive loving energy in return."

Grandma Patti went on to say, "You can also get loving energy from other things as well. Do you remember those beautiful crystals that I gave you for your birthday that you have hanging in your bedroom window? Every morning when you wake up and the sun shines through your window and the sunlight hits those crystals and sends little light rainbows all round your room, these crystals are a wonderful source of loving positive energy.

Some crystals can also be used to protect you from negative energies and feelings. Haven't you ever wondered why you feel happy in the morning when you wake up and see those light rainbows dancing around your bedroom? Think of those rainbow rays of light as me and others that love you sending you positive loving energies to start your day."

"Are you always with me in my dreams Grandma?" Jenni asked.

"Not always Jenni," said Grandma Patti, "but I am here when you need me. The secret is all you have to do is ask. Plus, there are many other loving spirits that are with you always and not just when you are dreaming. These loving kind helping energy spirits are what some call your Spirit Team!"

Jenni shifted her head to one side as if trying to better understand what her Grandma was trying to tell her about her Spirit Team. Jenni did not really understand what a Spirit Team was and what they were all about.

"I sense that you need me to better explain what and who your Spirit Team are and what they are all about," Grandma Patti said. "Your Spirit Team includes your Higher Self, angels, spirit guides, loved ones that have passed on, animal spirits, and other loving energy beings that are always with you to help you with your life's journey.

When you were younger, remember when you had your imaginary friend that you shared your thoughts and played with her when you were alone? Your imaginary friend is part of your Spirit Team that were there for you, all you had to do was ask. As you grew older and others told you that imaginary friends were not real and that you should not believe in them, in time you stopped believing.

  But your Spirit Team never left you, they were always there helping you and showing you signs that they were there to help you all along. All you had to do is ask and believe. Your Spirit Team is there to help you to make the right decisions, to help you better understand yourself, and to open all your senses to the loving energies that are all around you. It's all up to you to was ask and receive their loving guidance and help.

  Remember yesterday as you went downstairs for breakfast and you heard Bobby playing with his imaginary friend? Bobby is still open to talking with his Spirit Team and that is why he is still able to do so."

  "So, all I have to do is ask my Spirit Team for help," Jenni said

"Yes, that's right Jenni," Grandma Patti replied. "Asking is the first step and soon you will be able to recognize their help. Sometimes they leave little signs, a bird feather, a song you like suddenly comes on the radio, or you may even just get a strong feeling within you of the answer to the question you have asked.

Sometimes you will get feelings that things are about to happen. For instance, at breakfast you moved Bobbie's milk glass from the edge of the table. You didn't know why you moved it, something just told you inside to move the glass or it would spill. That is your Spirit Team at work. Do you remember when you were walking to school, and you suddenly called out for everyone to wait at the crosswalk without knowing why? Again, that was your Spirit Team's helping."

"Do you remember when I taught you that if something was bothering you and you were feeling a little stressed out, or if you were having trouble finding answers to a problem and you were to close your eyes, relax, and take a couple of deep breaths, how that would help? Well this is a way that you are actually asking your Spirit Team for help.

Have you ever noticed that when you do take the time, relax and take a couple of deep breaths, it seems like the answers to your questions or problem come to you? Didn't the answers to the pop quiz yesterday at school seem to come a little easier when you did this relaxation exercise?"

"Another good way to ask your Spirit Team for help is to find a quiet place, sit comfortably, close your eyes, take three slow deep breaths, and just sit silently for 15 minutes focusing on your breathing and listening to your heartbeat.

When you are ready in your mind, ask any question you want to know an answer to. Listen to any thoughts that come back to you. This is known as a form of meditation called mindfulness. There are many types of meditation, but this is one of the easiest types to start with. Also, when you have finished with this quiet time for yourself and go about your day, look for other signs that may have the answer to your questions."

"You are right Grandma, when I did that like you said at yesterday's math pop quiz, I was able to relax, and the answers just came to me!" Jenni proclaimed with excitement.

Grandma Patti went on to say, "Another way your Spirit Team will let themselves be known is through your sense of smell. When I am close to you, you'll be able to smell those wonderful pies and cookies that we used to make, especially during the holidays. I send you those smells of warm baking cookies to help you remember me, to let you know that I am near, and to give you love and protect. Other way that your Spirit Team can let know they are with you is by leaving you signs. You may ask a question or wonder about if you should do something or not. Your Spirit Team might leave you a feather that you may come across, you may run into an old friend that you haven't seen in a while that has some unexpected news, or you may hear a favorite song that helps make the decision. You might even find a shiny new penny on the ground as answer to a question you are thinking about at the time.

Sometimes answers come in the way of animals. I know you really like squirrels. A squirrel may suddenly show up in the yard or cross your path giving you acknowledgement to your question and to the answer that comes to you in your heart upon seeing the squirrel. When you are drawn to a certain type of animal, in your case squirrels, this may be to you what is known as your spirit animal, or what I like to call your "animal kin". A squirrel spirit kin is the sign of activity and preparedness. The squirrel reminds us of to keep a balance between work and play. So, while you are going through your day with school work and chores, a squirrel reminds us to take some time for yourself and play. This is why it is important for you to spend time with your family in the evening playing games or reading after a long day of school and chores. This creates balance in your life between work and play."

Jenni and Grandma Patti spent the rest of their time together walking in the meadow picking wildflowers and talking about their favorite treats. As the day seemed to come to an end, they found themselves at the end of the stream again were the dream began.

"Until next time," Grandma Patti said as she kissed Jenni on the cheek.

The dream faded as Jenni could feel the warmth of the morning light as it shinned through her bedroom window.

Jenni gave a big stretch and yawn as she began to awake. Suddenly she smelled something absolutely wonderful. Jenni threw back the covers, jumped out of bed and jumped down the stairs as she always did and gleefully shouted out.

"Pancakes!!!!"